Love Poems for the Socially Anxious
& Other Maladies

Sophia Iannuzzi

*Front cover art: Sophia Iannuzzi
Design and typesetting: Ted Wojtasik
Proofreader: Brayan Pacheco*

Acknowledgments

**The Alan Bunn Memorial Chapbook
Award Winner 2017**

*The Alan Bunn Memorial Chapbook Award Competition
was established in the memory of Alan Bunn
by David Bunn, Ellen Birrell, and Dr. Olena Bunn.*

ISBN-13: 978-0998194943
ISBN-10: 0998194948

SA
UNIVERSITY
PRESS

St. Andrews University Press

St. Andrews University
(A Branch of Webber International University)
1700 Dogwood Mile
Laurinburg, NC 28352
press@sa.edu
(910) 277-5310

Also by Sophia Iannuzzi

Sophomore Slump (2016)

For Ziggy.

♡

Table of Contents

refrigerator magnet poetry as a gift, untouched

though i explore this eternity,
my heart an old ghost,
your affections set fire to flowers
bring life to cold skin
and i burn
and i linger
in your
fever.

coincidences i.

i should like to crack
open your
skull

pull apart the tissue,
exist within the
neurons and the dura

bathe in the
fluidity of your
imagination

and explore the
inside of your
intellect;

such as the comfort
of an old book,
it feels like home.

coincidences ii.

we send
fragments
of our
patchwork souls,
exchanging
soundwaves,
pictures on screens,
words on pages,
with the hopes that
art
transcends
emotion
and can make
strangers
seem less strange

coincidences iii.

peculiar
isn't it
how in a car

with your
hand grazing

mine
traveling
beneath a dark
sky
with the
music playing
slow
we find
sunshine
in strange places

flowers

love is patience
  loving silence
love is kindness
  through the quiet
it does not envy
lovers on station platforms
mouths to foreheads
bone white knuckles grasping
lapels, cloth, skin –life by fists full
it should not envy the ones who love
freely.
so why does mine?

how it envies those spilling sentiments
like seeds in plowed souls
planting flowers
expecting growth
          honeymoon seasons harvest
hearts
plump and firm
          like honeydew melons
glazed slick in the sweetness of honeys
and saccharine sensibility

i must admit that
when we met there was frost.
though also, certainly, witch hazel
                         snowdrops
                         winter berries
                         camellias, *too*.
          that which flourishes in frost.

that, which can *grow* in cold condition.

the garden is sparse.
we have reached another november.
how can i be a camellia?

cómo se dice

a girl from paraguay
once told me that
english speakers are
inferior in their love
as they only have
one word for it.

those who speak spanish
have multiple synonyms
for love,
its symptoms,
and the level of said love.

i am filled with envy that my mouth cannot find the
language for you.

valentine's day

they slide on ice, one and two, two and one, like children
wrapped in winter coats/ with layers beneath the down
puffs causing their arms to stick out on either side. this is
how they keep their balance.

      love is just a pseudonym for feeling like
you're fucking crazy 24/7.
incoming call. 2am.

         one would give two
everything. the whole bag of kits. falconplumes, and
jackboots incloted... whatever two wanted from one, at the
drop of a hat. notebooks of sentiments and deep
confessions of adoration, though at the end of the day it's
just ink on a page, and one knows they will never make a
habit of a journal, despite wanting to.

"-- i'm sorry, i'm annoying myself when i say it but it's
like a stupid reflex."
           "you're

fine. i miss you too."

it's all too much and not enough at the same time. kerouac
said that, i think.

beach house insides with decrepit foundations fall apart
when the tides roll in, splintering from the salt which
sneaks inside crevices and slicks stairways to the point
where no one ascends. there's nothing up there, but i will
climb anyways just to check it out.

i tell him i'll call back later.

negative space

forgive me.
mirrors only mock
    it is difficult to see myself
so
    i have not met this version of me
 in quite some time.
i must think away fog to
make clear for conscience.

now i cannot feel
  if i gangle with incomparable height or
am mere inches tall.
 i cannot see
below the clouds
let alone what is above me
in front of me,
beside me.

forgive me.
is it i, who distances myself from
or,   maybe,   brain.
the mind is a separate animal, no?
                             you.

dark, to meet mortality's terms.
dark to know,
sherbet skies do not need me,

butterflies need no gilding,
the world will go and go and go.
i am not needed here as i once thought so.

i believe in wavelengths,
in vibrations,
that we dance on similar frequencies
children speaking through cb radios
try to connect to someone new
                 in self-diagnosed heartache.

if bumblebees were thought to be able to cross the planes
between this life and the next
       and back again
then   surely   i can exist in the same as you
even when it feels like you are in another
little do you know
i have tied red string from your mind to mine
your finger to mine
your toe to mine
our threads spanning continents.
it is there if you look.
stike it, sending vibrations through yarns to find me
i will answer   i will answer   i am here
can i reach you? do you read me?

waffle house

we woke up early,
rolling in opposites, side by side,
like a rorschach test.
we meet in the middle
but only occasionally.

                      "what can i get you,
baby?"
breakfast is on his mind, but i regret
to tell him there isn't much
of a choice in the area.

there is a salt shaker on the table during our first date.
unremarkable at first sight,
but his ocd says otherwise when he points its dented
tin lid away from him shyly.

the atmosphere works against him,
but his love of breakfast foods is stronger than his qualms.
                      "egg and cheese melt,
                      please."
his sanity is melting
his eyes track
the movement of goings on
behind the counter in the grill area,
making   jokes
 an assembly line of greasy
poking   holes

foods.
in   yolks.

the most important meal of the day
the most stressful.
food sates his stomach   purell sates his mind.

there is no softness in florida

he changes the florida sun, with its warmth that makes me
feel like sepia postcards of oranges and taxidermy
crocodiles from a lost era, and which does not reflect the
holiday season despite the christmas lights on palm tree
crowns. i remember pouting at these crowns, at the ocean,
at the sand. they never reflected my fatigue. there is no
softness in florida, only sharp angles and bright colors to
which i felt foreign. these days the sun does not cast such
long shadows, it is high, as we are. overcast kisses keep it
from hurting my eyes so i may see clearly. see, there are
swamps in my mind i do not visit anymore, like the
everglades they are rife with snakes and gators. thick and
overgrown with lush worry and the muck of insecurity.
knowing they are there is enough for me. i have spent too
long in these marshes that i have no desire to step into the
mud and wet my feet in silent sorrows. i will not eat the
fruits of the melancholy trees. in the florida of my mind he
rips up the splintered floorboards of the childhood home
lonesome made and replaces them in cherry wood, rich and
warm and smooth, easier for me to walk on when i return
to visit. much softer.

best served warm

you are hollow
let me fill you
you are hollow
sugar,   darling?
let me fill you
you are hollow.
i fill you.
fill me.
teacups,
pouring
sweet teas with cream
milky warm kindness
soothing stomachs
back and forth.
back and
forth and
back.
neither empty,
neither full.
me, covering the cracks
in your porcelain
with my hands,
and you, mine
so we do not spill
do not waste
let me fill you.
fill me.
fill you.

a joke

in bed, he is curious
he asks me what the female orgasm feels like
how it differs from male's
i tell him i was wondering the same thing
he does not laugh the way i hoped he would.

routine

step one.
i am freed
from crisp white linens which
bound my feet in their tangles.
like chains, only far more preferable.

step two.
reluctantly i tuck away,
previous night's dreams into a rucksack.
i leave remnants they left behind,
in the nooks of my eyes
a reminder of you.

step three.
i allow the wind to catch me.
guiding me through the motions of the day,
carrying me along, as i could never do
on my own.

step four.
i return in feverish haste.
in no time i feel as if i never left.
the only sign of my absence being,
another freckle, another spot—
a gift from a possessive sun.

finally,

as the rest of the world sleeps,
though the following hours are ours,
they are thin.
and before i know it, i must go through the steps again.
yet i would take these steps in thousands
                    millions
if i could make my way back to you.

phantom limb

should you leave me
i would have to saw
my left leg off at the thigh
as the crook
behind my left knee
belongs to the
stubble of your beard
which grazed its softness

but then
i would have
two limps

my hair changes more than the seasons

while my hair was still cut straight across my forehead and pale like lemon chiffon, metal ring in my nose, we fumbled with words in parking lots / i,with dark circles under my eyes, tired in many ways, same as you. you like my hair. i tell you it's a reflex. // there was magic in the violently mundane. /// cars parked, long drives, hour drives together. //// "look at you being my dream girl." ///// i did not dream then, there was no point in placeholders. ////// we rolled like stones between two cities, neither place fitting the two of us. in apartments with no furniture we filled spaces with our minds. /////// when i left i went red in the cold of winter, contrasting with snow like peppermint stipes, and you missed my chill in the south. i send you socks and twizzlers. //////// in a new year i returned, still in crimson, fitting for the blush of returned love, though it had not quite left. ///////// with the return of foliage and flowers, the saturation of my hair hushed to pale pinks like a prelude. and you left this time. i followed. if only for a little while ////////// summer began with fresh blonde locks, and i wondered if that was because i hoped to return to the beginnings of something, or if i was intimidated by the girl that lives below your bed in a shoebox. i settled with sun and sea and the distance between us, the latter two soon turned me blue. /////////// folicles turned brown as fall came and we collided again. I matched the brownstone and brick of the new york backdrop, a more polished look for your mother. I tried harder than was necessary. sometimes i wonder if it is difficult to love an assembly, never knowing who will show up. ///////////// i was gone again by september, leaving my roots alone as i explored my roots across the atlantic, *a roma*. my hair did not reflect my mood. i was not myself (certainly not to you) until i sat in pubs towheaded and content, save for missing you. ///////////// in the new year we end our push and pull. myself a reflection of when we began (sans bull ring), you never changing. maybe it's unfair, but i like you best that way. in fact, i may be envious.

to be asked what love is

two toothbrushes
in a cup
beside the sink
where there used to be one
and no cup

to let them in

i couldn't tell you how he cracked the code.
i couldn't tell you how he broke the seal,
or chipped away at the walls.
i couldn't tell you how he got past the booby traps
the moat
the hall of arrows
the pit of snakes
the mirror maze
the drawbridge
the interrogation room
my neuroses
the guard dogs…
but,

i could tell you how he makes me smile.

thirst

in spots where static once sounded
steadfast, i feel dreams
brewing. crazy notions
of lives we could live
if by chance you feel
similarly

laughter, a
drop of condensation
slowly slipping down a
glass of lavender lemonade
in sticky summer,
a fingertip at my spine,
pulling the thread of our fate
from the spool
longer and longer
and longer

smile.
bubbly cola
with extra cherry syrup
from the fountain,
sweet as sweet can be
popping when it meets
my lips
like static cling.
we cling.

no more static.
in sleep
despite your grumblings—
warmth, ecstasy,
soothes like richest
chamomiles
and me! a cookie
moving closer
soaking up the tea
of your person
leaching your warmth
a thief in the night.
imagine this, forever
if by chance you feel
similarly

i will read the leaves
of crumpled bedsheets
when we wake
and break away.
hoping for fortune,
and refreshment.

Biographical Sketch

Sophia Iannuzzi was a two-time St Andrews representative for the Gilbert Chappell Distinguished Poets Series for the 2015-2016 and 2016-2017 seasons. She has won multiple awards for her poetry. Though originally from southwest Florida, she now lives in Bar Harbor, Maine. When not writing, she can be found with her dog Oso—preferably on a beach.

www.ingramcontent.com/pod-product-compliance
Lightning Source LLC
Chambersburg PA
CBHW070050040426
42331CB00034B/2959